READ BETWEEN THE LINES

Edited by

Heidi Latronico

First published in Great Britain in 1999 by
POETRY NOW
Remus House,
Coltsfoot Drive,
Woodston,
Peterborough, PE2 9JX
Telephone (01733) 898101
Fax (01733) 313524

HB ISBN 0 75430 648 8
SB ISBN 0 75430 649 6

FOREWORD

Although we are a nation of poets we are accused of not reading poetry, or buying poetry books. After many years of listening to the incessant gripes of poetry publishers, I can only assume that the books they publish, in general, are books that most people do not want to read.

Poetry should not be obscure, introverted, and as cryptic as a crossword puzzle: it is the poet's duty to reach out and embrace the world.

The world owes the poet nothing and we should not be expected to dig and delve into a rambling discourse searching for some inner meaning.

The reason we write poetry (and almost all of us do) is because we want to communicate: an ideal; an idea; or a specific feeling. Poetry is as essential in communication, as a letter; a radio; a telephone, and the main criteria for selecting the poems in this anthology is very simple: they communicate.

CONTENTS

A NEW LIFE

I was the black sheep of the family
Caused by alcohol abuse
Whenever I got into scrapes
I made drinking my excuse

Until a girl that I befriended
Took me into church one day
And I became interested
At what the minister had to say

He talked at length of Jesus Christ
And how he had been our Saviour
I decided then to change my ways
And be of good behaviour

Now I am a different man
And a Christian life I lead
Drink is never in my thoughts
It's to Christ's way I take heed

Lachlan Taylor

THE HOSPITAL WAITING LIST

Chronic arthritis, there's an eighteen month wait,
I'm sorry Sir, to that my old mum can't relate.
Millions of pounds spent on statues and useless stuff,
While our National Health Service still haven't got enough,
Money to treat the old, the disabled and the poor insane,
All over the country, the picture's one of despair, it's all the same.
They have all got cut-backs and freezes, the nurses are in despair,
While we on the hospital waiting lists just wait and tear our hair,
In total frustration, because of the way the Health Service is run,
Never mind it's only seventeen months now to wait, my son.
To see the specialist who deals with your chronic lasting pain,
I'm sorry Sir you're not on the list, now what was your name?

Don Goodwin

VENUS
(dedicated to the one I love)

Placed in the arms of a dying whisper,
Love brings home the morning star.
Just so that the dewy eyes of dreamers,
Through misty veils of tears can still see;
      where they are.

Norman Royal

MY DAD

Who is this person I called my dad,
Who grew up so quickly from being a lad?

He was someone so special and loving to me,
If you had known him, you would surely see.

Son, husband, father, grandad and brother,
If he were your friend, he was like no other.

Always there when you needed his love,
And I'm sure he'll continue from heaven above.

Now he's walking straight without any pain,
And his love for us all is with us again.

To think that his goal he has now achieved,
To be with his maker we must truly believe.

Linda Garner

LOVE OF YOU

Love so utterly deep
Is my love for you
No matter how others try and reap
It will be completely useless in my earnest view

Sheer ecstasy flows within my bones
I am as a spellbound loon
My voice has a most special tone
When I can speak I'm over the moon

Your constant ravishing beauty
Is ever in my loving mind
It fills my very soul with a quantity
Of bounty, no one else will ever find.

Alma Montgomery Frank

A PROPOSAL

My darling Rose, from heaven sent
Who makes my heart beat with sweet content,
With hair of gold and eyes of green
Nothing so lovely in my life have I seen;
With eyes of an angel the grace of a dove
You fill my heart with a life of love;
I will love and cherish you all my life
And keep you from want, trouble and strife;
With these loving words, my love, I propose -
Please be my dear wife, my love, my Rose.

Lawrence Vandeldt

OUR HOME

We were a couple ready to settle down,
We wanted a home but not in a town.
Making up our minds on what to do,
We came across this sight with a beautiful view.
We did not ask what people felt,
We wanted our home on this green belt.
We went ahead we were so thrilled,
We got what was needed and started to build.
Toiling hard from morning till night,
With not another soul in sight.
We ate when we were hungry,
And rested when tired,
Thinking of our home we both desired.
Then came the storm that blew part of our home down,
I was in despair, should we have settled in town?
But when I looked at that beautiful view,
It was then that I really knew.
We have finished our home and settled in,
And planned our family soon to begin.
Our home is so cosy and central heated,
We have now got neighbours from far and near.
Sometimes now we live in fear,
You see we are two birds in a nest on a tree.

Christina Law

ETHICS

It takes an evil something
To wrack my leaden heart,
So under-used and so confused
And easy to outsmart.
An omnipotent something
That's free from right or wrong,
Who knows that I have no blind eye
And knew it all along.
It takes a bullish something
To tempt a man like me,
With premieres of derrières
I'd give my arm to see.
A brazen, two-faced something,
Aware of all my thoughts,
And when I stare it's always there
At all my last resorts.
It takes an impish something
To play around with fire,
To bribe me with dishonesty
And breed a hopeless liar.
A soul destroying something
That's going to change my life,
Its guarantee; adultery
With someone else's wife.

Allan Christian

SEEKING

Everything exists it's we who cannot see,
'seek and you shall find' could have been
a decree.

We must try to use the wonders of our brain,
for this may be our earth's best chance to
probe its space domain.

This could be the youngest universe which is
awake,
there must be lots of older races watching
the steps we take.

If we come across a race still running around
with clubs,
all we could do is take a look they'd only
like our pubs.

A race just like our ancestors
who roamed round wild and free,
would never go for all our taxes they would
not agree.

In the past we made new things
inventors did incline,
but, now we spend most of our time just
seeking to refine.

What secrets our old world must hold
buried beneath our feet,
new fuels better than we have
must we stay so discreet?

Where are our men of science
why just walk on a moon?
Our earth must have her secrets
still I hope we find them soon.

Jean Paisley

OUR REVOLUTION
(Dedicated to my home girls, you know who they are)

Together we're going to blow apart this pattern of silence
and start a revolution
Escape these rotating chains breaking free to find a solution
Shrouded in misery we can't live another day like this anymore
Our hearts have been burnt to the barren of the ground
and shattered to the core
We're going to start afresh in some enlightened place
untrodden and new
Where all these lifelong familiar grey clouds will turn
to passages of blue
Leave behind all those daily slave-like rituals and material objects
that hold unbearable tales within their possession
Make a pact and swear like a commandment
to stick by all our decisions
These bruises black and blue scattered inside-out
will never wash away or fade
Vibrations of remorse and guilt are as always promises
and lies that are never acted upon to bring about change
We've got to stop being on the receiving end
as someone's easy target and victim
Stop allowing the fear of aggressors and perpetrators
to continue with all the hurt they keep on inflicting
This time around we'll stand tall because we're not taking
or keeping the entrapped aching of pain locked inside anymore
Our lives for too long have been devastated and oppressed
and our physical appearances projected as images worn and torn
So from now on we'll persist to make our dreams
into some kind of composition of reality
Travel in need of no prayer just in the knowledge
that we are in the company of freedom
far away from all these bloodstained daggers of cruelty
Pick ourselves up from off the floor and make the thrones
to our existences and opinions be counted

Walk towards the moving sun where our destinations
from now on should be bound
Live the good life tasting the wanderess beauty and sight
of all that vision we once dwelled upon and longed for
Finally deciding to choose life over all the violent beatings,
ravaged suicides and inhumane deaths
This is the forward glance and march into our revolution
and this time we're going to reach out and make it.

Saheeda Khan

PERFECT DAY

The sun doesn't go away
on this perfect day,
The rain doesn't come
the day isn't glum.
I know he's looking my way,
I don't have a clue what to say
on this perfect day.
I know I'll remember this day
in every different way
In my heart this love won't end,
so rain stay away
I have nothing to say
except that this is a perfect day.

Gemma Eastwood

TROUBLED

When I feel lost
And alone
Don't think I can cope
With life all on my own
Trapped in my fears
Like a pile of rubble
I know at times like this
I'm feeling troubled.

R Blackwell

HEAR ALL ABOUT IT!

Feeling at a loss - so I read a book,
Very surprised - at how long it took,
It's a very large one - from a bygone age,
Mystery and love stories - on almost every page,
Learned so much - that I would not have known,
Showed over the years - how humanity has grown,
From simple start, through murder and recall,
This must have been - the greatest book of all,
Not just preaching - but with common sense,
Worth much more than - a fortune in pound or pence,
Got very tattered - rewritten quite a lot,
Never ever boring - because it has a plot,
Seems to have a strong grip - on my wrinkled hands,
Can't put it down now - consult it for my plans,
Can you guess the title - about people who once trod,
This land of ours - the 'bible' all about our God!

John L Wright

THE LOST SLATE

Humbled for I know my place,
Bewitched by the colour of night's tranquil grace,
Complying as true heart commands,
The familiar quarry challenges my mortal stance,
Unreal the blind revealed way beyond the gloom,
'O yes,' between grey clouds roams the offending moon.

Humbled yet to flatter my stare
   where the younger slate they tare,
Wooed by engulfing fever
   scolded by the rich affair,
Strike the chisel, dig deep for the past,
   bury legends in future pools of mistrust,
Young boys, mere children work faster still
   poor as in favours,
Fortunate to honour the hungry mill.

Humbled and lost by overwhelming peace,
'Beware,' offend thee not the ancient slate
   from eventual release,
All perfect dreams take time to mature
   true heart's cruel pain must endure,
'Be gone,' take flight, after dark must come the light
Shivering from the greater cold prospering from the past
   awakened from the fright.

Humbled am I drowning in slate sorrows alone,
   no greater teaching could I have endured,
For I willingly succumb to the dawn,
Lost slate of Nantele goes with my soul
   cherished for eternity
And I my veins flowed the dust of time
   when worthy I come back to thee.

Mansel Jones

CAN'T SAY NO!

God! She's ugly!
She asks, 'Do you want to come home with me?'
She smiles, teeth all dirty and broken.
I quickly try to think of an excuse,
I fail and say, 'Yeah, alright!'
I'm terrible, I just can't say no!

He asks, 'Will you help me?' I nervously check my watch.
Got to be elsewhere in ten minutes.
I look at him. He looks at me, the need for pity written all over his face.
'Yeah, OK. But not for long.'
Two hours later, I'm still there.
Getting to be a pain, this inability to say no!

'Dad, can you buy me this?'
'I really *need* it.'
I check the contents of my wallet,
Sadly devoid of cash.
'Can just scrape it, will have to go without, though!
'Yeah, OK son.'
Getting expensive, this inability to say no!

'Come on!' says the salesman.
Shoving this album under my nose.
'You *know* you want it!'
I do! I do!
But, but, but.
Oh! what the heck! I can handle it.
Going to do me in, this inability to say no!

My lover calls out to me.
Pulls me back to lay with her.
She looks at me and says 'Again?'
But. I'm tired, I think,
But say *'Yeah!'*
Got some good bits, this inability to say *no!*

Ivan J Peck

MY LAMENT

If I was a car with metal fatigue
I would be tossed on the mounting scrap heap.
If I was a vegetable gone to seed
I would replenish the earth's need, ploughed in deep.

If I was a snail in a cosy shell
I would be a meal for a feathered creature.
If I was a fox in a dewy dell
In the name of sport wiped off the country's feature.

If I was a dog with a role to play
Humanly destroyed when too old to work for my keep
If I was a cow, pig or sheep, I would have no say
Whether I be served up as a gourmet treat.

But I am human with feelings and failings,
Yet I feel no use, no reason to exist.
I have no desire, almost no cravings
Save one that always did exist.

So perhaps now I am at last gone,
Don't say nice things about me
That you couldn't whilst I lived so long.
Don't be hypocrites, be honest. Please let me be.

I can tolerate physical pain,
But I refuse to be sent on a guilt trip
Again and again.
You all had a choice and I am not to blame.

J Baker

FORGOTTEN LOVE

There came a day when I did despair,
after noticing my love was no longer there.
I searched high and low for what I'd lost,
never realising what would be the cost.
For to lose your love, is to lose your soul,
and without these things, life has no goal.
Then one day I saw a light,
within my mind it shone so bright.
I began to realise, my love was still there,
wondering why I'd forgot, with it being so near.
You never lose what you feel inside,
because it's from such feelings we learn of pride.

Christopher Roberts

UNTITLED

Got to go, got to run
Can live life with no fun,
Can only see black, can't see the sun
Got to save and buy a gun
My paranoia's got me under the thumb.

G Courtney

LAST CALL
(For my brother Richard with love)

Our cousin's out in hyperspace
constructed our glorious human race
every detail every flaw
they came in through our back door

All in aid of a better tomorrow
they sent an envoy to his sorrow
was it really worth it Jesus
you gave your life in order to save us

For we are worse
than we were then
can you honestly see
we could begin again

It may be too late I fear
Armageddon drawing near
all we are left to do is cope
wishing, praying, hope against hope

God forbid a drastic end
to heaven all our good souls send
love must triumph above all
listen human it's your last call

Deborah Hall

BIRD OF HOPE

Mid summer blues they called it when heat hung from the skies
Like wet and heavy curtain forfeit, unclean, and attracting flies.
Midday with heat debilitating darkness covered the sky,
Appearing clouds were thickening, and everyone heaved a sigh.

A coming breeze grew stronger, then a wind picked up the dust,
And darkness came much longer with each sweeping windy gust.
Lightening flashed with thunder heralding the coming storm,
Then huts were torn asunder as hurricane winds were born.

Rains came to parched earth with rivulets searching cracks,
And the eventual rivers gave birth to widening water tracts.
And still the rains poured down while day was black as night,
And waters rose above the town then all was lost from sight.

Hissing lightning flashed, the rumbling thunder roared,
All hope of help was dashed, and no human spirit soared.
Yet on waters deep too far away an Arc rode free and high,
And clutching waters were kept at bay as from that Arc a bird did fly.

Tommi E

WHY DIDN'T YOU STOP?

I am the hunted, I am the caged
I am the victim of man's rage.
I am the bear made to dance
I am the chimpanzee made to prance
I am the mink whose skin made your coat
I am the lion trophy that makes you gloat
I am the rhinoceros killed for my horn
I am the elephant from whom tusks were torn
I am the pheasant killed by lead
I am the tiger shot through the head
I am the salmon dragged from my fins
I am the duckling torn from my wings
I am the rat killed testing your drugs
I am the mole whose pelt made your rugs
I am the calf fed contaminate feed
I am the fox you made to bleed
I am the donkey you have made lame
I am the dog you kicked for a game
I am the rabbit testing cosmetics in vain
I am the horse you flogged for gain
I am the cat you choose to maim
I am the dolphin you wanted to tame.

I feel pain and I feel fear
Why is it human, don't you care?
Why is it my pleas you decide to reject
To treat all sentient beings with respect?

Haven't you thought in another life
You may had to bare such pain and strife?
I prayed man would have wisdom different from you
And treat all with compassion in all that he'd do.
Why didn't you stop - and look to see
The broken heart in such as me?

Anita Richards

NOUGHTS AND CROSSES

Rushing river of Wycoller village
hurrying with full volume of water
as if rushing to tell the good news, rage
over, ruthless period over, her
ability to be returned with love;
hell forced to recede to its bubbling place
as truth and joy erupt afresh, like dove
bringing evidence of real life, lets haze
of emotional and physical floods
evaporate, evil washed clean away.
Depression beat on essential good dooms
failure! Assertiveness keeps bad at bay;
whatever your cross Christ will hold you there
new life even at core of old; such care.

Robert D Shooter

FIRST TIME FUMBLING

We were delirious with lust as we kissed on my bed.
I knew it would happen from what we had said.
His hands got more anxious as he went for my bra,
and three hours later I was still counting stars.
I wasn't much better as I undid his flies
and caught all his bits - I can still hear his cries.
We were both saying nothing until I'd got off his kit,
and gasped at his wonder - it was never going to fit.
I got out a condom and watched him unroll,
then he clambered aboard to find the right hole.
As we pumped away I wanted to laugh -
it was all so awkward and we sounded so daft.
Then he kind of mumbled and I knew he'd come.
It was over so quick but I'd had such good fun.

Louise Gomersall

EPISTLE TO CHELSEY

Responding
To creation's need,
You Chelsey, into this world,
Are born.
Life's flame dances within you.
Newly scattered seed,
Welcome to
Your childhood's dawn.

May a loving family,
With patience and care,
Guide you wisely
Through these early days;
Themselves, learning
If they dare,
From the wisdom
Of your young ways.

Walk this earth with kindness and strength,
Follow your inner light.
A candle is set for you Chelsey,
You exist together.
It will burn strong,
It will burn bright,
It will burn,
Forever.

Patrick Allen

LOVESICK

Fly away beauty, on wings of a dove
Carry this message, to one that I love
Tell her I miss her, and how much I care
I miss all the good times, we used to share
Now we are parted by land and by sea
I wish she was standing, here next to me.
Many miles come between us, we are both all alone
Soon I'll be finished and returning back home
Till then I'll be faithful, honest and true
I shall write every day, and hope she will too
Fly away beauty, with this message I send
I shall love her forever, but for now I must end
Sorry it's so short, but it's breaking my heart
Thinking about her, each day we're apart
Remember to tell her, don't ever feel blue
Because darling forever, I shall always love you . . .

Gig

THE CANVAS

I gaze upon the blank canvas, dull and grey,
without enthusiasm.
The rivulets painted upon it are likewise grey,
with sepia splashes.
The sinister, sinuous movements
make continuously spiralling patterns
while colours merge together, some dark, some light
getting more frenetic as they run faster,
until mixed one with the other
they present a picture of deepening intensity
and the background of stark purple
becomes menacing and ominous.
I close my eyes as terror grips me
and wraps me in its unforgiving arms.
I am helpless in the path of the appalling hurricane
which is overwhelming and devastating
as it sweeps me to meet the black figure of death.

Paddy Jupp

THE DAY THE GOOD FRIDAY AGREEMENT DIED

Broken glass crunched underfoot
And flames chewed on the air
Acrid smoke clung to the scenes
Of devastation there

With rubble scattered all about
And blood upon the road
People staggered in confusion
Shock and panic glowed

Blue lights flashed in urgency
As sirens screamed and wailed
Evidence that politicians
Once again had failed

War, with a vengeance, had returned
Spat bullets at the crowd
And each explosive step he took
Reverberated loud.

Kim Montia

SUMMER RAIN

Summer rain fall down on me and
mingle with my tears,
Take my sorrows far from me and
drown my inner fears,
Merge with sun and cloud and spread
a coloured band above my head,
Trickle down beneath my feet,
Banish light and glowing heat,
Whisper gently in my ear as you pass me by,
Take me in your gentle stream so I no longer cry,
Sprinkle on my solemn face, restore my gentle smile,
Soak my hair, replenish me and stay
with me a while,
Rest down upon my dry surround,
Gently seep into the ground,
Leave me sodden, cleansed and free,
Retreat to the place where you should be.

Kelly Pidwell

FIRESIDE PICTURES

Not for me the harsh flashed light on walls
From screens square shaped and fed from aerials.
Eyes noting images from other lands, and ours,
Scenes of great beauty, stark horror, comedy, plays.

My memories are of red fires rosy burning
Whose glowing embers wait each winter evening
For ashy, baked potatoes, chestnuts roasting
And we with youthful expectation, waiting.

Our fingers moulded shapes and curious images
Resembling birds, cats or scary witches
On walls where firelight shadows pranced
Until the embers fell and bright flames danced.

Pam Gibbons

DEMENTIA

Through the tangled threads of my memory,
I search for the person I once was.
The future is a void into which I dare not look,
For fear of drowning in a sea of nothing.
The past is a grey misty curtain
Which sometimes parts, showing glimpses
Of faces and places. Bringing to me
For an instant, a spark of recognition,
Fanned into a brief flame of remembrance
Of fragments of my life.
I struggle to hold the pictures in my mind,
But the flame dies and the curtain closes,
Enveloping my brain like a blanket of thick fog
And leaving me once more perplexed.

Who are you, you who tends to my needs,
With a face that is strangely familiar?
Tied to me by either duty or love,
Are you my daughter, my sister, my mother?
Are you the baby I once bore
And cradled on my knee?
Or am I the baby you once bore,
Now grown to an elderly monstrous child?
And you no longer the mother
But the warder of this prisoner,
Who is sentenced to a life of confusion,
With no remission for good behaviour.
I sit here with my terrified smile, wondering
What I have done to deserve this fate.

Patricia J Harding

CUSP

The old year is passing.
As it fades into the night
The new year is standing in the door.

To some, the change brings promise,
To others hope or fear,
Some barely notice new for old at all.

To some the old year drained them,
Piling burden upon load
And the weight made footsteps heavy, glances low.

Perhaps for them, the new year,
Though it shines but dimly now,
Will strengthen as the days grow warm with sun

And wrap their weary shoulders
In a canopy of love
That will shelter them whatever may befall.

Jeanette E Burden

MONDAY AFTERNOON

Waiting at the bus stop in the wind,
Talking about Cumbria and the countryside.
You said, 'Nursing homes cost you a fortune.
Sometimes you've got to sell your house.'

I said, 'Some people live till they are ninety,
Full of love and wit. giving a helping hand
Doesn't cost a lot.'
Holding your hand as you get on the bus.

Kenneth Mood

WHY WRITE A POEM?

Express your feelings,
Happy or sad,
Think your thoughts,
Write them down.

Stories are too long,
Riddles are too short,
But a poem is perfect,
Just right.

Rebecca Daniel (12)

TOP OF THE CROPS

Some say I'm British to the core
But what that means I'm not quite sure
Am I then a 'Granny Smith'
Of greenish skin and firm beneath
Or soft and sweet like red 'Delicious'
With no propensity for being vicious
Or the Cox's orange I'm now gripping
With everyone thinking I'm a 'Pippin'!
P'raps a 'Blenheim' - flying high
Spurning lesser mortals - 'getting by'.
A toffee-nosed twit loving 'Royal Galas'?
And OBEs in the Queen's front parlour
With 'Spartan' qualities to the fore
In battles won in days of yore
When Drake and Raleigh sought to be
The leaders in 'Discovery'
Or now a 'Laxton' - *once* 'Superb'
Reduced to poetically indifferent blurb
Well
I'm just an 'old fruit' from a 'family tree'
Who for centuries fought to keep Great Britain free
And
For the future, now, and in days gone by
Great Britain's the 'apple' of *democracy's* eye.

John Elias

AFTERDAYS

I can smell the pond
Where I walked with my mother
In blue sandals and mud.
Visits to Bob and Mamie,
In whose kitchen, and with toast,
My first poached egg.
In the car my father,
I with traffic lights on sticks;
Going different colours
As the stickiness increased.
Tranquil distance, seeping
Into thoughts of afterdays.

Carolyn Oulton

ENDEAVOUR

Created in a chapter - captured the imagination
he strives to conquer every clue
a precision in English - education dark blue
the times crossword, adds to the challenge
solutions written in - by nib not biro
a connoisseur in fine wine - opera - and books
real ale - classic cars - and life
stories from the ancient world
entwined mysteries and murders, begin to unfurl
the dreaming spires, always inspire
it's a rainy night - case still unsolved
let's call it a day - home - goodnight
turns the key to his own private world
new day - new clues - soon all will be clear
opera tells of good triumphant over evil
the answer lies before him - though hidden in veil
so try as you might to unravel this man
he is - an Oxford man - through and through.

David Charles

MENISCUS

Two eggs on a wartime plate,
No comment no debate,
All knew the recipients' fate,
Their mission to start from that date;
Our gratitude lingers even this late.

To be dropped behind enemy lines,
Resistance and sabotage by underground designs,
A call for extra courage in high adventure;
Brave persons by their very nature,
Shown the more so during their capture.

The Millennium Dome with its proclaiming face,
Phoenix like from derelict land and waste,
A salute to a new milestone,
The leap from the past into the hopeful unknown;
A beacon signalling into outer space.

A cooked egg on a breakfast plate,
A rich yellow cupola rising from white foam surround,
Not for long will it captivate and be around,
So what can be gleaned from a thing so underrate;
How can it celebrate anything profound?

From a beginning through liberating wars to a new millennium,
We are part of an unrolling continuum;
Thankful we should be that appetite was made to wait,
Till the original egg was allowed to incubate.

Eric Ashwell

THE TV

What are they showing on our screen
Gross obscenities, that's what I mean
Our children fixated drawn and misled
Not by others but by the television instead.

What happened to the normal soaps
Nowadays we all have high hopes
That out children will actually see
That it's not all true what's on TV.

Children beaten, people possessed, that's true
What is the television teaching you?
What's happened to education and good fun?
What has the media actually done?

The television is full of violence and pain
That will actually drive our children insane
What happened to the good old-fashioned movie
That I and all others thought was quite groovy?

Stop and think what you are showing our young
Some of these images are so very strong
Bring back all the pleasure to portray
That television may give us good will one day.

Annie

NIGHTMARE

In the depths of my mind a recurring dream
Always to haunt me so it would seem
Thirty or so years it was there
Waking my sleeping a horrific nightmare

Trying to find a reason for this
Convinced a former life did exist
Now knowing it to be a childhood fear
Silly I know for we were loved very dear

Behind a door lies my fear
A bed a door the horror was near
I know I must enter here within
But the feeling of fear creeps over my skin

Discussing my thoughts of living before
I told of the horrors behind the door
There's a bed made of iron standing therein
Next to a door my fear would begin

'It's Harry's bedroom' my sister said
'Don't you remember the old iron bed?
The door was the cupboard we could hide in
It was terribly big quite frightening'

As she describes it all becomes clear
The nightmare I've had year upon year
No longer the nightmare to face every night
Just in remembering dark turns to light

Not knowing what hid behind that cupboard door
Was the reason for horrors of that I am sure
Understanding now why bedroom doors I don't close
A part of my childhood in me arose

Susan Goldsmith

GHOST

Come to the place between heaven and death
One last time tonight.
Come and walk the earth again
Before you walk into that light.

Come gently, come softly
I shall not fear thee, as I did at first.
Envelop me and smother me
I'll breathe you in till my lungs could burst.

Come lay down beside me
Once again, leave your impression there
Let your heavenly scent linger
Swirling sweetly in the air.

Come pass through this body, entwine my heart
So I may feel your soul within me
Let me wish it there for ever
Before you set your spirit free.

Alison Glithro

PERHAPS

It's standing in the corner
It's dusted every day
It takes away the talking
It keeps us both at bay
So, why do we put up with it?
We sit there every night
Why don't we get rid of it?
One day, we just might.
But then, what would we talk about?
No football, films or soaps
No TV dinners on a tray,
No Les Dennis jokes.
Perhaps I'll keep on dusting it
Watch just BBC 1,
Learn to talk a little bit,
But not when TV's on.

D M Harrington

BEYOND CONSCIOUS VISION

Though visionary dreamers can be boring in extreme
I'd really like to share with you my very special dream
Wherein I saw another world - a better one than this
Where warmth and gentleness abound and everything is bliss;
Where nothing is impossible as wishes all come true,
And those you loved in times gone by wait fondly there for you;
A land of glittering palaces and flowers that never fade,
And animals are friendly for they needn't be afraid;
Where fishes jumping cheekily will never come to harm
And birds sing with abandon as they perch upon your arm.

Your loved ones will prepare a place for you to join them there,
For life on earth is transient, as everyone's aware,
And though you sorely miss them it will only be a while
Before your eyes will open to the welcome of their smile;
The sparkling crystal ocean laps on golden miles of sand
Where friends and former enemies are strolling, hand in hand;
Whatever are the grievances that fester in your veins,
What cruel words and actions cause recurrent mental pains,
Just persevere with courage till you reach that sweet reward
Where all may be forgiven, and where everything's restored.

Rosemary Yvonne Vandeldt

PHANTOM NURSE

As I sat down late one night
I felt a cold shiver go down my spine
Which gave me quite a fright.
As I looked yonder over there
As folk sleep in the calm night air
I saw a woman dressed in white
She was hovering from bed to bed
Then suddenly disappeared from sight.
Should I yell - should I shout?
Or stay calm, keeping quiet
For she did me no harm
This lady from long ago
Must have seen tales of woe
When she herself was there
Tending others in her care.
I wonder what life she led?
Must have been more noise at night
Caring for soldiers who did fight
Now the white lady can rest
Here folks she has blessed.

Sheila Waller

THE HOODED FIGURE

I ask, imagine if you will
a country lane winding the hill
The moon is bright on Stonestyle Lane
as I am walking home again.

The owl is hooting in the wood
then there . . . a figure in a hood
That field I forced myself to pass
There *it* was . . . a cow munching grass.

Valerie Ovais

SPIRITS OF THE DEEP

Now a twisted broken torso of human endeavour -
she spends her resting days on an ocean bed . . . for ever -
The mass consciousness that swarmed her decks
an echo of the turmoil, violence, disorder and vex.

Freshly painted lifeboats, no one to heave
sit the well-to-do clientele, yet to leave.
'Women and children first' authoritative voice
order or disorder, to mass . . . no choice.

Bow to stern the peoples fend
falling, jumping a downward trend
Children scream a torrid cry
eyes, glancing eyes as she touches the sky.

Her stern adrift, lost souls in flight
Titanic submerges out of sight
An aftermath of screams tear the air
lifeboats glisten and people stare.

Bobbing bodies adrift, alone
sacred their motions far from home
She cannot sink she cannot die
or so they thought, why oh why . . . ?

Andy Rosser

HOMELESS

I walk the streets, in the bitter cold, I'm homeless,
This chilling, biting wind gets into every bone,
I watch people go by, they couldn't care less,
They sometimes laugh as they make their way home.

Because I'm out here on the streets, all alone,
Does not mean I am idle, or I've just given up,
Things have happened that I could not condone,
Life can be so unkind, for the weakest to cope.

I walked the streets with my family, not long ago,
Then things got on top of me, I started to drink,
I lost everything and everyone, it's easy you know,
I still walk the streets, but I started to think.

The drink was frozen out of my system for good,
I have gone to those unknown angels of kindness,
Yes, still I walk the streets but I see as I should.
I now help others who wait in the cold to die - homeless.

John Shanahan

DEATH OF A LIFEBOATMAN

Bending mind and will, steeling emotion
To hold nothing back, not weighing out love,
Giving no thought to call to devotion
To duty - more, the worth of life to prove.
A life for ten lives no less an expense.
Yet even those lives are as thin as floss,
Not to admit is to live by pretence.
Yourself you gave in the waters of ice
While comrades bent backs and murmured their prayers
And hoped that your chance for life would come twice.
The search took them home with the saved - and cares.
A home bereft, grieving, but child and wife
Must struggle on, their lives cut by death's knife.

Ardis Gaylor

CHOICES

When I survey my landscape bleak and cold,
I think about what passes for a life.
Remembering forgotten realms of gold,
Before I fell into the Vale of Strife

Those far-off days, I stood above the clouds,
A queen of choice and liberty I tow'red.
Above the grey mundanity of crowds,
On that green hillside, coloured options flow'red.

Bright flowers which festooned the paths of youth
Are shrivelled now and blacken on the vine.
All pathways now are shortened by life's truth,
And dead end mazes, twisting, life define.

If I could redesign life with my pen,
I'd tear the manuscript and start again.

Jennifer D Wootton

A SONNET TO FATHER

Did you ever love me like I loved you?
You lived in a completely different world.
My love remained ever shining and true,
But like a dying leaf, your love was curled.
My love danced like moonlight on the water,
And through storm and calms in the dead of night.
But you knew I was your only daughter,
Yet you jumped like shadows out of the light.
And although time changes and we grow old,
And the sun must light up the morning dew,
Please do let me, father, out of the cold,
As I seek to know you, again, anew.
              Thus do ponder over what I have said,
              And let us try now before day is dead.

Lydia Ayres-Hyman

GRANDMOTHER

When insignificant forget-me-nots
creep up the hill, I will remember you.
It was a special day you told me lots
about a boy who picked those flowers too.

But then we must move on to other spots.
So many flowers in your garden grew,
and we had heard of some disastrous plots
to cut the grass which would destroy them too.

We did our best to save the daisies all:
the pretty girls in white and boys in red.
Not one should unworthily lose its head.

You loved the violet small, the tulip tall,
the pelargonium on the window sill.
But most forget-me-not. I never will.

Susanne Södergren

I AM HERE

A quest bequeath I'm on loan
Another season in this form,
In moderate terms I'm satisfied
To pass my time in sacrifice.

I'm here with you both night and day
Passing each other on the way
No recognition light our path
No memory stir the joys once shared.

The form you knew is gone to rest
Where daisies grow to take the test
Of life on earth where all was balm
Before trial and stress breach the calm.

I'm here beside you on the road
Sharing the burden of your load,
Beside the current of the streams
Rich amber flow to fairer dreams.

I'm here to conquer inner thoughts
Of pleasant moments, lessons taught,
To cast aside insidious deeds
Learn to give as much as take.

I'm here before you in the wake
When stormy clouds assail your stride;
Transparent views turn darkness light
And morning dawns sunny and bright.

I'll be here when passions stir
The air breathed upon your wreath
And you recall the dreams we shared
When you once portrayed me 'Dear'.

Zeedy Thompson

THE PANE

Peering intently through the glass pane,
All I could think of was getting warm again.
I felt how cosy and happy they must be
Not giving a worry or thought for me.

How I longed for something to eat,
And the cold to go from my frozen feet.
I had walked miles and miles with nowhere to go.
To be back home I longed for so.

I began to doubt if I was a human being,
People passed by me without even seeing.
Except one who said in a loud voice,
'Don't feel sorry for him, he made his choice.'

I wandered on distressed and debased,
No one knew the horrors I faced.
Long cold nights all alone,
Love from a bottle is all I've known.

I can't take this life for one more night
The way to warmth is within my sight.
I kiss my love just one more time.
A bottle through the window, then warmth through a crime.

Kathleen Barron

NOW I UNDERSTAND

I watched as slowly down the valley flowed
A trickle, then a stream and then a flood
Repayment of a debt for too long owed
But not long now before the taste of blood
I close my eyes, yet through my lids I see
More clearly now than I have ever done
The infant, child and adult that is me
Each day, just one more battle to be won
And feel a peace like nothing I have known
With strength to share the burdens of the weak
For too long I had thought I was alone
Now look, at last, within for what I seek
And know that when I really need to share
I only have to pray, to find you there

David C Hannibal

FOOTSTEPS TED HUGHES CONTINUED

A silent view through the curtain of life
A voyeur observes the cloud-laden sky
Quandaries that trouble the perturbed mind
Still rivers run deep in meandering flow
The wan moon peeps from behind her cloudy veil
Trees silhouetted against a backcloth of night
Casting long deep imposing shadows
A bird of the night makes a shrill call
The wind whispers quietly through the branches
The birds astir with melodic chorus
Dawn breaks tentatively to clear daylight
All humanity adrift on a becalmed sea.

Francis Arthur Rawlinson

THE WISDOM OF YOUTH

The questions you ask
I answer
but you know so much more,
from football star to disco dancer
upon the kitchen floor.

You autograph the walls
and run when you should walk,
although you are so small
we listen when you talk.

The pictures you draw
are placed
you do not set a price,
in the office pride of place
'My dad is very nice.'

You build the world a city
with lego in your hands,
it's really more's the pity
that the child leaves the man.

Justin Le Fort

PLEASE MISS

Please Miss - what can I do?
I know that one plus one is two,
And four plus three does equal seven,
And six add five becomes eleven.

But when I try to do subtraction,
I find my brain goes out of action,
Please Miss - what can I say?
I don't know how to take away.

Please Miss - I want to cry,
You've taught me how to multiply,
Twelve times four is forty eight,
Five twos are ten, and no mistake.

But when you say we must divide,
I wish that I could go and hide,
Please Miss - I need a hand,
Division, I don't understand.

Please Miss - I like trigonometry,
It is, to me, quite elementary,
Obtuse, acute, or equilateral,
Triangles to me are natural.

But algebra! Oh dear! I fear,
I cannot do, get nowhere near,
Please Miss - if A plus B is C,
Why not call them, one two three?

James W Sargant

SANCTITY

How diverse are the creatures of the night
A lapse upon their sanity
Can cause abysmal blight
To self dispose could be an answer
Willing to go - no enhancer
Cooled by chilling cold stream thoughts
Eternal life cannot be bought
Infatuation for unknown
Forgetting life's seeds once were sown
Back to our origins now
All our lifespan will allow
In death alone
A crumbling bone

Billy Adair

TEAMWORK

Well you have got to be joking
It's a bit overcrowded in here.
We will have to get an extension,
Excitement buzzing - what an atmosphere!

Now that everyone's working together,
Gosh we have run out of space.
But we've now spread across the world,
Our aims to make this a better place.

So the world has joined together,
Let's thank God for progress.
Love, understanding and beauty,
Quality and quantity at its best!

Ann Beard

THE MORNING AFTER

Down a green lane hemmed with hawthorn
Lies a pool of water gleaming
Where a grove of ancient oaks
Has been a thousand years a-dreaming,
With a hollow at its feet
Where we lovers used to meet
Beneath Selene, palely beaming;

But well I knew such stolen rapture
Only leads to sorrow.
And I would not risk the loss
Of all that I might beg or borrow.
Yet, now sitting here alone,
I would give everything I own
If yesterday could be tomorrow.

J C Fearnley

MY LONGEST TRUE LOVE

My true love once had a heart that gave me so much love.
I had this heart and I really truly enjoyed his love.
Now he doesn't have a heart any more, because he isn't now my love.
He is now with someone for ever and for good.
He is not my true love any more, but he was my first serious true love,
That I will never, ever forget.
I don't think he will find a love like me again
I don't think I will find a true love like him ever.

S J Gorman

FEES OF LIFE

The heavy autumn fees that trees must pay,
Brings to the mind, Godiva's lady wife;
If they should wish to see another May,
Dressed to the hilt with shades of colour rife,
Strip to the trunk and chance the cold and rain,
And all is bare to every Tom who peeps,
Not turned to stone, or have destroyed - their brain;
They miss the shame when Abele sadly weeps,
Though artists show the proof for all to see,
The indifferent glance moves on and on,
And just a few will stop and feel - Maybe!
With concentration, miss those who have gone,
And understand, not only man must pay
The fees of life, but all who see a day.

Carolyn Long

PAGE IN THE PAST

The lamplighter makes his journey homeward bound
Through gaslit streets of swirling smog
His pole in hand, his job is done
Till morning comes to do his round
The yellow smog cuts off the breath
And stifles the night air
It chokes the townspeople with its fumes
Until their health's impaired.

When morning comes the sun breaks through
The curtain lifts again
Milkman comes with horse and cart
His shire decked out with brass
Followed by the rag bone man
Who calls out his patter
As his wheels rattle past
The scene is set
A London street
A child, no more than three
A day gone by
Now a page left in modern history.

Jenny Anderson

TO JESSICA FRANCES BUNN

Sweet babe, darling one,
Memories of times long gone
You bring to me.

The songs you hear
My own late mother dear
Sang to me.

Your mother's sweet voice
Croons just the same choice
I sang to her.

Those soft lullabies
Bring deep sleep to your eyes
In dreamless repose.

Alice Hall

A THUNDERSTORM

Tingling sensations, electrified air,
wind hushed to silence, e'en nature lies calm!
Uneasy stillness pervades all around,
calamity brewing seems everywhere,
creatures lie cowering in your coppice there!
Forecasting instincts of danger or harm,
(including animals, down on the farm!)
Thunderstorms pending, their fears they declare.
Lightning illuminates now darkened skies,
Cloud-crashing thunder vibrates on the ear.
Rain, now torrential, the parched earth supplies
God's gift of rainfall allaying drought fear.
Earth lacking moisture soon withers and dies,
Thank God these showers replenish each year.

Marjorie Williams

COUNTRY FARE

The breeze plays softly o'er the rough hewn moor
Stirring the heather masses as they lie
Like Nature's carpet on uneven floor,
Resplendent in the warmth of sunlit sky.
And through this rustic panorama winds
An ancient road with just around its bend
A coaching inn where many a traveller finds
The goal for weary feet to slowly wend.
Inside its age old portals, burning bright
A welcome fire with ruddy burnished glow,
Old oaken beams and glinting lantern light
And conversation's amicable flow.
The hills, the plains and rural signs declare
Fine attributes of simple country fare.

Doreen F Jackson

LOVE SONGS

Do you remember those old
forty five records we used to play?
There was a time we would just listen
to those love songs all day.
Today they don't get listened to
as much as they used to do.
I've kept all of those old forty five records
in an old cardboard box.
Please don't ask me why.
After you left and went away
your favourite record was badly scratched.
I searched those old record shops just
trying to find a replacement copy for you.
I even sent a letter to a local radio DJ asking him
to play your favourite love song on the radio,
with a simple dedication just saying I still love you.

K Lake

I Wait

I wait, for you my love, to come to me and envelop me into your arms.
Come to me and grace me with all of your charms,
until you find me, my beloved, my life is dark and empty.
Darkness is my light, the weed is my flower and the thorn is my tree.
Perhaps instead, should I search for you?
How many distant lands shall I cross, how many oceans mustl I swim?
Never knowing, will he find me or must I find him?
Oh, where are you? I search endlessly and travel far,
to the ends of the world or nearer in the car.
I shall look high and low.
And I will go . . .
Into every crevice and ravine,
to the highest mountains and hills in between.
My heart fills with despair and sorrow,
for who knows the day I find you,
I know not, will it be tomorrow?
I live in mourning, I live in death,
The day I find you, I shall draw my first breath.
So, come to me my love, for I am a half and you are the other,
. . . together . . . a whole.
Anguish and sorrow are my only true friends,
The day you come to me, will be the day the pain ends.
No more agony from every pore,
And that will be the day, when I begin to live,
and wait no more.

M M Wheaton

BOOK OF LIFE

Take each day, a step at a time
Write your book of life, line by line
Live your life, for good or worse
Write your book, by chapter and verse.

Be careful of errors, that may cause you strife
For all is recorded, in the book of life
From the sins you've committed, to the ones that you think
The book of life's not written in ink.

You may live with patience, you may live with rage
However you live, goes in page by page
It's all down to you, how your story narrates
As you stand before God at the heavenly gates.

For each and every soul has a tale to tell
It may be told badly, could be told well
This is one book no man can amend
From the very first word to the last word. The End.

David Strauss Steer

LOVE'S LUNACY

Have you ever known the pain of too much love?
It fills your chest and constricts your throat
When you speak what was an audible voice
Is released into the sound of a croak.

Have you experienced the fear of too much love,
The fear of letting go
Truly allowing someone to come in
And let what you're feeling show?

Have you had the joy of too much love
The kind of lunacy,
When everything seems so perfect,
And you're ecstatically happy?

Have you spoken in the language of love
The one where you always agree?
Your conversation transforms the meaning of I
Magically into a we.

Have you ever known this kind of love?
If not, be careful, you see,
It can happen when you least expect
And it affects you permanently.

Sonia Tennent

RENNIE

You came to me
like a fresh spring breeze
a welcome hand
that led me through the trees

A smile so warm
a soul twined with mine
such love I embraced
in those arms of thine

And on your warm chest
my head will always be
the comfort of true love
in my eyes you will always see

I will love you forever
my saviour, my angel, my friend
two hearts entwined forever
that will beat in love till the end

My lips will never tire
of embracing your warm kiss
and just knowing you are by my side
is the deepest, warmest bliss

Susan Stewart

LATE AT NIGHT

It's now, late at night, when the darkness comes,
When I miss your voice, your eyes, your touch,
When the time ticks slowly, slowly by,
When I want, I want so much.

The dark makes the time stretch so,
Makes the bed seem big, so cold,
Makes me feel the ice of loneliness,
Makes me dream of words I was told.

Of promises, of lives, of futures,
That never happened, that never came true.
Of love that never flourished, of a heart that died,
That changed from vibrant red to coldest blue.

It's now I wait for daylight, for the dawn,
For the days that never can be,
Sometimes I wonder about you,
Whether you ever dream of me.

I doubt you do, I doubt you ever did,
But I know you acted, so very well,
Misled me, made me believe you, enticed my trust,
Dragged me to this burning, burning hell.

I loved you with all my heart,
You lied to me, pretended, broke me in two,
Maintained the spell, spun your web,
Then carried on, a dalliance, that's all I was to you.

I hope one day to find another,
A lover, a man who cares, who's honest, who loves,
Who stays with his heart for ever and ever,
Not one who changes his mind as often as his gloves.

Patricia Cunningham

LOVE AND ART

After great despair about the future
Our relationship entered calm waters.
The purpose of life is love, and not need,
Sometimes I have mistaken need with love.
I worship beauty, and love is beauty,
But love can never a prisoner be,
It comes of its own accord, in freedom,
I must patiently await love's return,
That is the wonder of love, as it will.

I need to analyse my attitude
To emotional ties, that is my quest.
To be more patient towards my lover,
He is the beauty I truly worship,
With or without a physical regard,
I love him, it alters not, is the truth.
When he leaves his haven after the storm,
However long his period of doubt,
If he calls I will hear him and rejoice.

I do not believe he has dismissed me,
But I am in the recess of his mind,
My course is to accept until love comes
In all its force, more stronger than before,
If I pursue it will increase the gulf,
Whereas understanding, above all love,
Will win through in the end. In the meantime,
Recreating our times in poetry
Will be worth achieving during this phase.

Betty Mealand

THE FEAR OF FAILURE

I've ran with pain
It never left my side
The enduring mind
Uplifting me with pride
As I edge towards my goal
My pain becomes greater
But a feeling of greatness
Overrides me the doubter.

Warren Brown

MISTAKES

Mistakes, yes I've made a few
Some small, some large but most in the middle
A few caused me to be in trouble
But nothing very serious
But there was one, one that changed my life
I don't know if it was for the better or the worse
That mistake was long ago, when I lost you
Sometimes this is good, I have freedom
Sometimes this is bad, I wonder what might have been
I don't know if I miss you, I never knew you
But I don't think I would change anything
You see, I like the way my life is
If I changed things long ago
My life wouldn't have been the same
I don't know what would have changed
But I know it would have been different
Would it be easier or more difficult?
The answer to this I would never know
Mistakes, I've made a few
And I wouldn't change a thing.

Rebecca Moorhouse (16)

DESOLATION

Tie up the emotions
With unseen threads of grief
Savage winds of want blowing away the senses,
Leaving no tenderness,
Empty eyes that look into the
Darkness of this void,

Grey dawn breaks, remnants of yesterday's
Nothingness, stretching into eternity,
Grasping, swirling, mists
Within a mind ravelled, for want
Of your sweet love.
Come my dear heart, tie up with tattered thread
Our ravaged time, where I in desolation wait
The usurper of our love,
Proclaim my life in thine
To live again.

Elizabeth Lydle

SOLITUDE

Someone turned the light out,
Now I cannot see,
I have to use my instincts
And tread more cautiously.
Someone changed the blueprint,
Now I've lost my way.
Do I follow how I feel
Or close my eyes and stay?
Someone switched my duty,
Now I'm so confused,
I do not know the answers
To things I always knew.
Someone ripped my heart out,
Now I feel no pain.
Do I try to resurrect
Emotion once again?
Someone tried to deal me
Cards I couldn't play,
Should I have gone along with them
Or maybe had my say?
Is someone there to shield me,
Keep me safe and feel my need?
To hold and to convince me,
I don't need fear to believe.

Caroline J Sammout

NOW WINTER NIGHTS ENLARGE

Now winter nights enlarge
The number of their hours,
And clouds their storm discharge
Upon the airy towers.

Let now the chimney blaze
And cups o'erflow with wine,
Fierce winds try to raise
This old homestead of mine.

Log fire glowing throws its light
Flames leaping in the air,
Storm continues with its fight
Raging on out there.

We sing our song, and sip our wine
Contented with our lot,
Put our trust in the Divine
And soon storm forgot.

Soon a sound could not be heard
In the old homestead,
Too tired out to speak a word
We all retired to bed.

J Naylor

NINETY-EIGHT

Ninety-eight, at last has gone, a year I care not to remember
to Huntington's, my darling wife, her life, did so nearly surrender
They said have your children, they said the problems would not exist
they did not have to face our kids, to say with them,
                                        Huntington's has kissed
Both now facing, a much shortened existence
to come to terms, with intolerable ignorance
At thirty-five, stamped rejected, your working life,
                                        no longer proceeding
an early age Huntington's bitter test, you are falsely, reconcile
                                        to conceding
Inequitable Industry, put you out of work, but not for you Dispensation
criterion, is to be severely maimed, to qualify for compensation
Not for you Insurance, the risk is far too high
your amounting debits, will reach, far into the sky
Little choice on how you live, undoubtedly, the system will try to fool
harsh reality will reign supreme, the Secretary of State, will
                                        financially rule
A human can die at the hand of another, the media, gives its
                                        fullest attention
fifty thousand souls, will perish, at the hand of Huntington's,
                                        never get a mention
My heart is so heavy with all this pain, in thirty-five years,
                                        not a thing doth alter
we have the knowhow, and technology, to stop this human slaughter
Demoralising, degrading, a long slow lingering death,
                                        hard to comprehend
most will spend their ailing days, to die without a friend
I have never before seen such hatred, heaped upon victims,
                                        with injudicious persistence
locked away from public conscience, victims' own families,
                                        in denial of existence

The age old condition Huntington's Chorea, will never fit the rules
despite the unstable appearance, are human and not besotted fools
We can only imagine the anger, we can only guess,
at how they really feel
Hope, liberty, dignity, and life we have stripped, from the to steal
The sighted cannot see, the deaf to distant calls
help could be available, is surrounded, by impenetrable walls
Few will ever notice, most will never see
families struggling in a hell, from never to be free
Your eyes amass with life's own tears, brave face for all to see
you are left only dreaming, on just how life might be
I have two darling angels, they alone give me hope
Kay Gordon, and Debbie Turner, without them I could not cope
they help me through my troubled times, caress my wearisome fear
these two angels of gold, are always there, to wipe away my tear
I'm honoured, to have cared for Huntington's, they have more guts,
than you and I
they cope with a parent inflicted condition, are ridiculed to the day
they die.

H Beena

FREE EXPRESSION THE TRUTH AS I SEE IT

M Is for the *millstone* of the European Community around
Britain's neck.
I Is for the *illegal* emigrants they flood into Britain every day.
L Is for the *legalisation* of homosexual rights for sixteen year olds
what a sin.
L Is for the *legions* of men and women who have died for peace
in vain.
E Is for *Euro*, we British want to keep the Pound.
N Is for the promises the British Government *Never* keep.
N Is for *Nuclear*, the bomb the Americans would like to drop
on everyone.
I   Is for the *insulting* behaviour of people everywhere every day.
U Is for the *Uprising* of Jesus and The Christian Faith within
your souls.
M Is for the *Mess* that man has left this beautiful world in, a world
of sin.

Were you to live three thousand years, or thirty thousand years,
remember this.
That the soul, life which a person can lose, is that which he or she
is living at this moment.

Believe in The Lord Jesus Christ.

Dohmnall Le Gai

GIFT OF CARE

There came the gift of care
And a gentle soothing stare.
From then on I would heal
As I learned to begin to feel.

The years had left their mark
Frequently they were dark.
But slowly came the sunshine
As mellow, as mellow wine.

I'm no longer afraid as I was
'Cos
I've been taught to live on my courage
I've been taken on a loving voyage.

So with this gift of care I blossom
I hope forever free of asylum.
I hope forever I get the care
Even if I don't know where.

Denise Shaw

MISTY MEADOWS

Winter's howling winds,
saxifraga flowers
red, speckled blue,
bitter cold with a sharp snap.
Marsh marigold flowers
in pockets of
sandstone gleaming
crevices snowstorms
brings life to a
standstill autumn
chilly morning
forest of changing colours.
Spectacular gold leaves
silver, yellow
blown to piles of
hibernation bedding
for hedgehogs,
for the long
cold sharp bitter
winter ahead.

Alan Hattersley

PLEASE PHONE

I hate it when you phone me,
With your voice so soft and sweet.
I can almost feel you present,
Beside me on the seat.

I hate it when you phone me,
It makes me want to cry,
I can almost smell your perfume,
And see the twinkle in your eye.

I hate it when you phone me,
Just before you go to sleep,
I hate it when you say goodnight,
It almost makes me weep.

I hate it when you phone me,
And say sweet nothings in my ear,
I hate it when you phone me,
I just wish that you were here.

David C Cushley

VULGAR?

If I won the Lottery
Without any toil or strife
What of this world
Should a Lottery claim my life

A vulgar way of living
In an endless luxury
If not a sin
I ask, would this all - 'Be me?'

Would I trust myself to stay
My own person with completeness
But wait, oh - worse -
Would I trust others even less?

Never a money person
- To be a Lott'ry winner
A cuckoo - land
Yes I would feel - a 'viewed sinner'

There'd certain to be envy
And perhaps old jealousy
I could not cope
I'd pray to God to release me

If I won the Lottery
A conscience would develop
Should a cash-load
Around me envelope

I'd get sick of 'a Christmas'
Occurring every day
I'd be so glad
to give it all away

Existing with everything
In contrast to my colleague
- Win a Lottery? -
I prefer to stay in my own league.

Barbara Sherlow

IS SILENCE GOLDEN?

Love lovers love
Oh! Oh! La La
Before we forget we are human
You are a woman I am a man
A human being
Oh yes oh yes
I am a woman you are a man
Created to love
To make love and be loved
To respond and reciprocate love
Lovely loveable loving enlivening tender tenderly
Delightful delighting delights
Colourful colouring colours
And most of all above all
To listen to see to hear to express to taste and to deny
Silence is golden
For lovers most of all
Long to hear to utter to feel to whisper in harmony
Harmoniously peaceful in peace
I love you I love you.

Ghazanfer Eqbal

MODERATION OF MODERNISATION

Television by skill of man is beneficial in so many ways,
Can give pleasure can teach, explain things
Keep us in touch with modern topics,
News programmes each day.
Television in many respects is in some way
Controlled by adults who know many pleasures
You do yourself exist,
That are more physical, don't keep you sitting down
Though occasionally this can be bliss.
There are many people who for one reason or another
Cannot live a physical everyday life,
For whom television is a boon, gives them so much pleasure,
Which otherwise they could not get involved with
Quite so much, which is really nice.
We have an on also off control which takes a twist of your hand.
I think modern people today are very sensible,
Are not complete television addicts,
Many watch it to relax after a day's work,
So it can be really grand.

Victoria Joan Theedam

LOVE'S FOOL

Trembling: you're naked, eyes closed, I'm blind,
Satin on your skin makes the dark hairs rise.
Oh! So slowly! So softly! I'm so kind.
I tie the black ribbon around your eyes.
Laughing at me you turn your face away,
Sensuous, exciting, a lover's game:
It's a new one, you think you'd like to play,
Tempting, mysterious, never the same.
And now you can't see me while I hurt you,
(I could cry if I see your face in pain).
A sharp knife in the back cuts through and through.
You scream, you writhe, and I can laugh again.
Oh! It's painful, it's bloody, but I don't mind;
I close the door, leaving love's fool behind.

Jessica Yeo

WHY SO MANY MARRIAGES BREAK UP!

There are too many facts the young people today
Do not feel that they are responsible.
It makes them sad but do not grasp what they did!
Remember we do live in a free and liberated society
Where the morale has gone completely out.
The responsibility and the commitment
Does not mean a thing in this day and age.
Too much sex before marriage, people live in sin
Many lost the sense of reasoning.
Life today is no more so simple like it was in the beginning.
Today everything is so complicated, people feel so frustrated.
They cannot compete, they are squeezed.
They feel so lost, they are exhausted.
This society needs a big help from the top
To guide them to find the way, gain the morale
And the responsibility, and live happily with their family.
The law must be changed to make a good sense to all of us.
If anyone is married they must be responsible.
It must be the first priority, by a strong law
In this lovely country England.

Antonio Martorelli

UNTITLED

And I can dream
I am alive
You care
Your love
Your tender words
Your prayer

And I can dream
That if I died
I would not have known
All your soft tender eyes

And I love you all
For being there
And especially
For being you, in your golden stare

I love you all
Especially because
Because because
You care.

Dennis Manly

NO ENCORE

Quit when you're winning, is that what you'd say?
And always leave them when they're wanting more?
No backward glance as you went through that door
And left us all. Just so. The following day
News fell upon us like a poisonous spray
And drenched us, pierced us to the core.
I came to you. I was a visitor.
I didn't even touch you where you lay.
They'd done a careful job; you looked quite calm
And undisturbed; perhaps even amused
By what had taken place that summer's day.
Surely one last farewell would do no harm?
But no, it seems an encore's been refused;
You left us wanting more. That's how it is. Okay.

Trevor Millum

AM I

Am I going mad,
Am I really sad,
Am I really bad,
Am I really ill,
Do I need a pill,
Is there something
wrong with me,
Something that the eye
cannot see,
When put to the test,
Why am I acting different
from the rest,
Why does it all seem so hazy,
Am I really going crazy,
Or is it just my current
woes,
That made me not know
where to go,
And this is just the way
I cope,
And have lost track of
the hope,
That there is a light at the
end,
And maybe something
nice just around the bend.

Teresa Wild

GHOST

I am floating, I am glowing
I am like a human being but I am a ghost.
People don't know how I feel.
Some can see me but I'm not real.
I float about behind your back,
I flap about, then I attack!
I make a noise like a wolf that howls,
I come out at night and sing to the owls.

Lauren Sammout (6)

WHAT WE KNOW

I can see my life
gone by
as stepping stones across
a way.

I remember what
was once
a phase, or slot, a place
of mine.

I remember
innocence
as something I would
gladly know.

Unaware of
obstacles
stigma, judgement,
complicate.

But innocence once gone
is gone
and found again it
cannot be

except, perhaps as
magic flash,
an unexpected
saving grace.

In torment, suddenly
we know
we may return to what
we were.

In anger, suddenly,
today,
it may help us to find
a way.

Kevin G Thompson

LOOKING AT LIFE

Looking at life
One could say that we're here today and gone tomorrow
And that we only achieve
if we truly experience love . . .
and sorrow;
Indeed one can borrow and steal
but it doesn't really help you a great deal.
A perfectly born babe
beautiful in every way
is then crucified; doesn't die
but lives on painfully to stay.
A wife loving her husband
he then dies and goes to the promised land
after only months of marriage
a tragedy, like a death from a crash in a train carriage.
But she lives on and crushes the sorrow
and for another man goes to follow.
Why do some experience such grief
and others do not experience it even in brief?

T A Saunders

SEA BREEZE

Caught unaware,
By your ominous stare.
Fill my lungs
With the poisoned air.
Cut out my tongue,
Frightened to speak,
Because I'm too weak.
I don't care
What they say.
They destroy my life
As I cut the edge
Of my frozen soul,
With a blunt knife.
She bleeds,
Like a quiet whisper,
As I disappear,
Beneath the cold waves,
Hugging myself,
With only God near.
I don't want to be saved.
I need to nurse my anger,
As the hatred breeds,
Like a virile disease.
Yet they can do as they please,
For I will emerge,
From the deep dark ocean
A distant man,
But able to find
The lucid truth,
Of the sea breeze
As it brushes,
Behind,
My fragile mind.

Graham Hardie

AFTER A WHILE

After a while,
You learn the subtle difference, between holding a hand, and
Chaining a soul.
And you learn
That love doesn't mean leaning, and company doesn't mean security.
And you begin
To learn, that kisses aren't contracts and presents aren't promises.
And you begin
To accept, your defects with your head held up, and your eyes open,
With the grace of an adult, not the grief of a child.
And you learn
To build all your roads on today, because tomorrow's ground
Is too uncertain for plans.
After a while
You learn that even sunshine burns, if you get too much.
So plant your own garden, and decorate your own soul,
Instead of waiting for someone to bring you flowers.
And you learn
That you really can ensure . . .
That you really are strong.
And you really do have worth.

William Price

ETERNAL RAPE

The light went out of my life
One dark November night
As I walked home from town
I got such a terrible fright.

A man had crept up behind me
And threatened me with a knife
He said if I screamed or struggled
That he would terminate my life.

I was then pushed to the ground
And of my clothes he did divest
My body then was violated
Before he stabbed me in the chest.

From my wounds I did recover
But I daren't go out my door
For I've now become agoraphobic
Because my courage I can't restore . . .

Irene Hanson

MY ISLAND

The sandy grain upon the shore
Will it be here for evermore?
The wind blowing through the trees
Like a wind chime and a silent breeze.
My island. My home.
I'm here on my own.
The water flowing down the stream.
I'm wondering if it's just a dream.

L M Goodwin (12)

DANGEROUS RUBBISH

Not so very long ago
Men laid down their lives, just so
You and I could speak and say
What we believed in day by day
They tried so hard, just to preserve
The spirit, plus the sacred nerve
That makes us different, when we stand
Alone, to save our native land
It was an idea, that we should
Be free to worship, so we could
Do these things without the fear
Of persecution, or be near
The torture chamber, or the cell
Or other horrors straight from hell
But things have now begun to change
And media tempers in a rage
Can oust a man from work and home
And cause him miseries unknown
To editor, or vicious snout
Who bring about a losing bout
And talents welcomed once as rare
Are cast aside without a care
And so we watch this great display
Of powers by people held in sway
The sale of newsprint will reward
The efforts of this savage horde
We think that we are safe and sure
They'll never knock upon our door
For we are far removed from fame
And we thank God; for being sane
Away from all this worthless kin
And stuff the papers in a bin.

Edna Hunt

MY SHADOW - MY ANGEL AND ME

I have a little shadow, he follows me around.
We travel to many places together, yet he doesn't make a sound,
He is the kind of friend that's truly loyal you see,
He listens when I talk to him and never questions me.
I find his presence a comfort in times of trouble and strife,
I know he'll stay right by my side throughout my lonely life.
So many times I've talked to him, to thank him for being my friend,
My life is so much happier now, I hope it will never end.
The friendship I have with my shadow is what I'm referring to,
Just confide in him your worries and he'll be there for you.
The Lord gave us a guardian angel to see us through each day,
To guide us through the trials in our lives in his own caring way.
I know not what the future holds, but one thing I know for sure,
So long as it's my shadow and me,
There's nothing we cannot endure.

My shadow - my angel, and me.

Michele Simone Fudge

FLOATER

I'm just a poem that's floating around
Hoping to be excepted
Will I end up in an anthology, well bound
Or will I be rejected?

Will the judges smile, or will they frown
I know poems are thoroughly inspected
I won't get upset if they turn me down
It's only to be expected.

I'd like to see myself in print
I suppose it's my main objective
But I'm just made of pen and ink
And I feel right unprotected.

Fred Tighe

JOURNEY'S END

A single bar illuminated the darkened room,
Throwing a ray of light through an air filled with gloom,
Tinted with the stench of decaying flesh,
That made me gasp with every breath.

Moulded in the chair lay the remains,
Of a friendship I had once gained,
Her open eyes no longer saw my world,
Mouth a gape, silent without a word
Skin blackened with congealed blood,
Body stiff like a plank of wood.

Wishing I'd been there to say my last goodbye,
I used my hand to close her eyes,
Taking some time to be there alone,
Holding a hand that was nothing but bone,
Feeling the coldness of her corpse,
My heart filled with grief, my tears with remorse.
Down upon my knees I said a prayer,
When her journey ends I hope she'll be happy there.

Pauline Uprichard

LETTERS FROM SIS

Tender notes played
for me
in cheerful words,
political rampages, social diatribes,
small greetings tucked into precious gifts,
history lessons, life lessons,
testimonial wit,
poems.

Her poems cross lines,
ambush with sardonic humour.
Her poems cross oceans,
encourage me to swim.

Where ink has dried
I see that time and space
loves us not less.
she winks from the page
fakes a posh accent
and pats the bum
of a passing dignitary before making
her latest constitutional request.
A pressed violet falls like a sigh into my lap.

I save them all:
words, violets, sighs.

The post comes and
my heart leaps in recognition.
Our souls collide in thankful embrace.
I would change only
that she were here.

Julie Glaser

SUBMISSIONS INVITED
SOMETHING FOR EVERYONE

POETRY NOW '99 - Any subject,
any style, any time.

WOMENSWORDS '99 - Strictly women,
have your say the female way!

STRONGWORDS '99 - Warning!
Age restriction, must be between 16-24,
opinionated and have strong views.
(Not for the faint-hearted)

All poems no longer than 30 lines.
Always welcome! No fee!
Cash Prizes to be won!

Mark your envelope (eg *Poetry Now*) *'99*
Send to:
Forward Press Ltd
Remus House, Coltsfoot Drive,
Woodston,
Peterborough, PE2 9JX

**OVER £10,000 POETRY PRIZES
TO BE WON!**

Judging will take place in October 1999